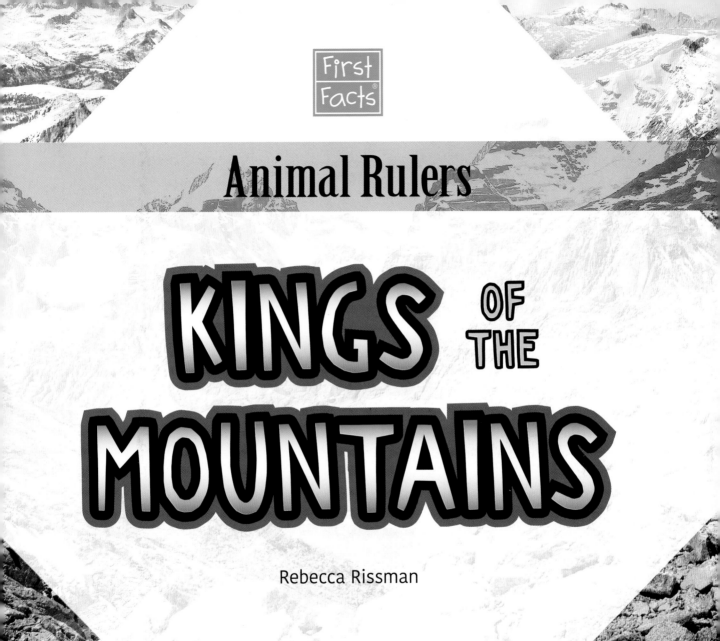

First Facts®

Animal Rulers

KINGS OF THE MOUNTAINS

Rebecca Rissman

raintree

a Capstone company — publishers for children

Raintree is an imprint of Capstone Global Library Limited, a company incorporated in England and Wales having its registered office at 264 Banbury Road, Oxford, OX2 7DY – Registered company number: 6695582

www.raintree.co.uk
myorders@raintree.co.uk

Edited by Adrian Vigliano
Designed by Kayla Rossow
Picture research by Kelly Garvin
Production by Kathy McColley
Originated by Captsone Global Library Limited
Printed and bound in China.

ISBN 978 1 4747 4864 3
21 20 19 18 17
10 9 8 7 6 5 4 3 2 1

British Library Cataloguing in Publication Data
A full catalogue record for this book is available from the British Library.

Acknowledgements
We would like to thank the following for permission to reproduce photographs: Shutterstock: Ammit Jack, 13, Baranov E, 11, Dennis Jacobsen, 19, Dennis W. Donohue, 15, dptro, cover (top left), FCG, 17, leeloona, cover (top middle), Matt Jeppson, 21, Michal Ninger, cover (top right), My Good Images, 5, Petr Kopka, cover (middle), Photo West 7, robert cicchetti, cover (bottom), Scott E. Read, 9; artistic elements: Shutterstock: Alexander Yu. Zotov, Alexvectors, blambca, By, Gallinago_media, Galyna Andrushko, iconizer, Les Perysty, nanovector, Nikolay Se, Petrovic Igor, oorka, robert cicchetti, steffiheufelder, Yoko Design

We would like to thank Jackie Gai for her invaluable help in the preparation of this book.

Every effort has been made to contact copyright holders of material reproduced in this book. Any omissions will be rectified in subsequent printings if notice is given to the publisher.

All the internet addresses (URLs) given in this book were valid at the time of going to press. However, due to the dynamic nature of the internet, some addresses may have changed, or sites may have changed or ceased to exist since publication. While the author and publisher regret any inconvenience this may cause readers, no responsibility for any such changes can be accepted by either the author or the publisher.

Contents

On top of the mountain

High in the mountains, a few animals rule. Giant wings swoop. Sharp fangs bite. Deadly claws swipe.

Mountain rulers have **adapted** to control other mountain animals. They have few **predators**. They travel large distances. Some are skilled hunters.

adapt change to fit into a new or different environment
predator animal that hunts other animals for food

Grey wolf

A pack of grey wolves howls in the night. These speedy predators are after their next meal.

Grey wolves live in Europe, Asia and North America. They use their sharp teeth and strong eyesight to **stalk** other animals. Wolves can kill animals as big as elk, bison or moose. A single wolf can eat up to 9.1 kilograms (20 pounds) of food at once!

stalk hunt an animal in a quiet, secret way

Grizzly bear

Grizzly bears live in North America. Most of the time, grizzlies are peaceful. But they are aggressive and skilled hunters.

Grizzlies are huge. Males can weigh over 454 kilograms (1,000 pounds). Their size does not slow them down. Grizzlies can run at about 48 kilometres (30 miles) per hour! Grizzly bears rarely attack humans. They only attack to protect their food or babies.

Mountain lion

Mountain lions live in North and South America. They have sharp teeth and claws. They are quick and **agile** climbers. Mountain lions are sneaky hunters. They hide and watch their **prey**. Then they pounce! Mountain lions run up to 80 kilometres (50 miles) per hour. They can also jump up to 12.2 metres (40 feet) to catch deer, coyotes and raccoons.

agile able to move quickly and easily
prey animal hunted by another animal for food

Andean condor

Andean condors live in South America. Their huge **wingspans** can reach up to 3 metres (10 feet). Andean condors don't usually kill prey. They eat already dead animals, such as sheep and llamas.

Andean condors build nests on high cliffs. Few other animals can survive at such heights. This means the condors have few predators.

wingspan distance between the tips of a pair of wings when fully open

Fact! Human activity threatens some mountain rulers. Andean condors are threatened by human hunting.

Snow leopard

Snow leopards live in Asia. They
are strong and fast. They can jump
15.2 metres (50 feet) in a single leap.
Snow leopards are **fierce** predators.
They use their sharp claws and teeth to
hunt. They can kill animals up to three
times their size.

fierce daring and dangerous
endangered at risk of dying out

Fact! Snow leopards are **endangered**. Sometimes, humans hunt snow leopards for their thick, beautiful fur.

Mountain gorilla

Mountain gorillas live in Africa. They
eat plants and are usually very gentle.
But these gorillas rule the mountains.
Mountain gorillas live in groups.
A large male called a silverback
leads each group. If a silverback feels
threatened, he pounds his chest and
roars. Sometimes, he even attacks!
Silverbacks punch, shove and bite.

food chain series of plants and animals in which
each one in the series eats the one before it

Fact! All living things are part of a **food chain**. Mountain gorillas are at the top of their food chain. This means they have few predators.

Wolverine

Wolverines have sharp claws and deadly teeth. Wolverines usually hunt small animals such as rabbits. Sometimes they hunt prey as large as caribou! Wolverines live in North America, Asia and Europe.

Wolverines are dedicated hunters. They will travel up to 24.1 kilometres (15 miles) a day for food. They will also dig to eat animals hiding in **burrows**.

burrow tunnel or hole in the ground made or used by an animal

Timber rattlesnake

Rattle, rattle! A timber rattlesnake makes a warning sound. It may be about to attack! Timber rattlesnakes live in North America. They have a deadly bite. Their sharp fangs contain **venom** strong enough to kill large animals. However, timber rattlesnakes usually eat small birds and mammals.

venom poisonous liquid made by an animal to kill its prey

Fact! Timber rattlesnakes only attack humans if they feel threatened.

Glossary

adapt change to fit into a new or different environment

agile able to move quickly and easily

burrow tunnel or hole in the ground made or used by an animal

endangered at risk of dying out

fierce daring and dangerous

food chain series of plants and animals in which each one in the series eats the one before it

predator animal that hunts other animals for food

prey animal hunted by another animal for food

stalk hunt an animal in a quiet, secret way

venom poisonous liquid made by an animal to kill its prey

wingspan distance between the tips of a pair of wings when fully open

Find out more

Books

Gorillas (Animals are Amazing), Kate Riggs
(Franklin Watts, 2015)

Grizzly Bears (Bears), Molly Kolpin
(Capstone Press, 2012)

Snow Leopards, Jen Green (Collins, 2014)

Websites

**www.dkfindout.com/uk/animals-and-nature/dogs/
grey-wolf**
Find out more about the grey wolf.

**gowild.wwf.org.uk/regions/africa-fact-files/
mountain-gorilla**
Learn all about mountain gorillas on Go Wild, a World
Wild Fund for Nature website.

Comprehension questions

1. Describe the way a silverback fights. Why does this behaviour make it a fierce animal?

2. Explain some qualities that help animals rule their habitat. Think about animals that live in extreme habitats, or animals that are very good hunters.

3. What do you think would happen if any one of these large predators were to die out? How would their disappearance affect the habitat?

Index